W9-CHH-484

THE DENVER BRONCOS

BY

MARK STEWART

Content Consultant
Jason Aikens
Collections Curator
The Professional Football Hall of Fame

NORWOODHOUSE PRESS

CHICAGO, ILLINOIS

151 Library
Kate Bell Elem. School

Norwood House Press
P.O. Box 316598
Chicago, Illinois 60631

For information regarding Norwood House Press, please visit our website at:
www.norwoodhousepress.com or call 866-565-2900.

PHOTO CREDITS:
All photos courtesy of AP Images—AP/Wide World Photos, Inc. except the following:
Topps, Inc. (6, 14, 20, 21, 34 right, 36 top, 37, 40 both, 41 top & 43);
Author's collection (34 top, 35 left & 41 bottom).
Special thanks to Topps, Inc.

Editor: Mike Kennedy
Designer: Ron Jaffe
Project Management: Black Book Partners, LLC.
Special thanks to: Susie Hall, Michael Florman and Amanda Jones.

LIBRARY OF CONGRESS CATALOGING-IN-PUBLICATION DATA

Stewart, Mark, 1960-
    The Denver Broncos / by Mark Stewart ; with content consultant Jason
Aikens.
        p. cm. -- (Team spirit)
    Summary: "Presents the history, accomplishments and key personalities of
the Denver Broncos football team. Includes timelines, quotes, maps, glossary
and websites"--Provided by publisher.
    Includes bibliographical references and index.
    ISBN-13: 978-1-59953-066-6 (library edition : alk. paper)
    ISBN-10: 1-59953-066-X (library edition : alk. paper)
    1. Denver Broncos (Football team)--History--Juvenile literature. I.
Aikens, Jason. II. Title. III. Series: Stewart, Mark, 1960- Team spirit.
    GV956.D4S74 2007
    796.332'640978883--dc22
                                2006015333

© 2007 by Norwood House Press.
All rights reserved.
No part of this book may be reproduced without written permission from the publisher.

The Denver Broncos is a registered trademark of PDB Sports Ltd.
This publication is not affiliated with the Denver Broncos, PDB Sports Ltd.,
The National Football League or The National Football League Players Association.

Manufactured in the United States of America.

COVER PHOTO: Jake Plummer and Rod Smith congratulate each other
after a touchdown pass during the 2005 season.

Table of Contents

SPORTS WORDS & VOCABULARY WORDS: In this book, you will find many words that are new to you. You may also see familiar words used in new ways. The glossary on page 46 gives the meanings of football words, as well as "everyday" words that have special football meanings. These words appear in **bold type** throughout the book. The glossary on page 47 gives the meanings of vocabulary words that are not related to football. They appear in ***bold italic type*** throughout the book.

Meet the Broncos

For some football teams, success comes quickly. Others have to wait a long time. The Denver Broncos know about waiting. They went nearly 30 years before capturing their first championship. During this time, the Broncos played in some unforgettable games and found a way to build a great winning *tradition*.

Broncos football is exciting football. You never know when the team will suddenly explode for a long touchdown or an amazing defensive play. The Broncos look for players with this kind of game-changing talent, and the fans love them for it.

This book tells the story of the Broncos. They brought **professional** football to the Rocky Mountains in the 1960s, and reached the top of the NFL twice in the 1990s. They had their ups and downs in between, but they never stopped trying for the championship.

Jake Plummer (left) and Wesley Duke greet
Mike Anderson (middle) after a great run.

Way Back When

Denver fans have always loved their teams, but for many years the major sports leagues overlooked the city—it was just too hard to get to. With the arrival of jet airliners in the 1950s, Colorado was no longer "too far away." In 1960, Denver was one of eight cities to join the **American Football League (AFL)**. The Broncos were started by Bob Howsam, who was better known as a baseball *executive*. One year later, the team was bought by Cal Kunz and Gerry Phipps. They loved football and wanted to bring a championship to Denver as soon as possible.

This did not happen right away. In fact, for most of the 1960s, the Broncos were one of the least successful teams in football. They had many good players during this time, including Lionel Taylor, Eldon Danenhauer, Gene Mingo, Frank Tripucka, Floyd Little, and Rich Jackson. But it was not until the 1970s that the Broncos began winning more often than they lost.

Under coaches John Ralston and Red Miller, Denver built a strong defense called the "Orange Crush." It was led by stars such

ABOVE: All-Pro lineman Eldon Danenhauer
RIGHT: Frank Tripucka, the team's quarterback in the early 1960s, carries the ball against the New York Titans.

as Tom Jackson, Louis Wright, Lyle Alzado, and Randy Gradishar. The team's offense featured many exciting players, including Haven Moses, Riley Odoms, Otis Armstrong, and Rick Upchurch. In 1977, the Broncos went 12–2 and reached the **Super Bowl** for the first time. They lost to the Dallas Cowboys, 27–10.

During the 1980s, Dan Reeves took over as coach. With strong-armed quarterback John Elway leading the Denver attack, the Broncos returned to the Super Bowl three times, but lost each time. The team's luck finally changed after Mike Shanahan was hired to coach the Broncos in 1995. He built a new team around Elway and young offensive stars Terrell Davis, Shannon Sharpe, and Rod Smith. The Denver defense was led by Steve Atwater, Bill Romanowski, and Neil Smith.

The Broncos finally put it all together and won back-to-back championships. They beat the Green Bay Packers in Super Bowl XXXII and the Atlanta Falcons in Super Bowl XXXIII. Elway retired, but the team's winning tradition carried on, as the Broncos continued to be one of the best teams in football.

LEFT: John Elway scans the field for a receiver.
RIGHT: An overjoyed Terrell Davis lifts the Super Bowl trophy for teammates and fans to see.

The Team Today

The Broncos have created a formula for success that always gives them a chance to win. The team looks for smart, quick **blockers** and strong running backs. The Denver defense specializes in hard tackles.

The Denver offense features a lot of tricky plays. The Broncos fool teams into thinking the ball is headed one way, then suddenly it is being run or thrown in the opposite direction. The Broncos have become so good at what they do that they no longer need star players. Anyone with the talent and desire to play the team's special brand of football is likely to do very well.

When fans take their seats at a Broncos game, their eyes never leave the field. Although the team's goal is to wear down opponents over 60 minutes, at any moment a player on offense, defense, or **special teams** might make a breathtaking play. That is what the fans have always loved about the Broncos, and always will.

Jake Plummer and Mike Anderson rejoice after a Denver touchdown.

11

Home Turf

The Broncos play their home games at Invesco Field at Mile High. One section of seats that circles the stadium is exactly 5,280 feet—or one mile—above sea level. Invesco Field opened in 2001. It was built very close to where Mile High Stadium once stood. This had been the team's home field since 1960.

The Broncos play in an enormous stadium that offers the latest in technology, including two huge scoreboards. But it also *incorporates* features that remind people of "old" Mile High Stadium. For example, the seats are very close to the playing field, and players can hear everything the fans say. Outside the stadium stands Bucky Bronco, a 27-foot model of a horse made of *fiberglass* and steel. Bucky used to sit atop the scoreboard in Mile High Stadium.

INVESCO FIELD AT MILE HIGH BY THE NUMBERS

- *The Broncos' stadium takes up 1.8 million square feet of space.*
- *Workers used 130,000 bricks when building the stadium.*
- *The stadium has 76,125 seats.*
- *The Broncos beat the New York Giants, 31–20, in their first game at Invesco Field at Mile High, on September 10, 2001.*

Invesco Field is a sea of orange and blue every time the Broncos play.

Dressed for Success

The Broncos' first uniforms were left over from a college all-star game played in the late 1950s. They were brown and white with yellow trim. In 1962, the Broncos began wearing the combination of red-orange, white, and blue. They still wear these colors today, although the blue is much darker.

The team logo has always featured a wild horse, or bronco. In the 1960s, there was a football player riding a bucking bronco.

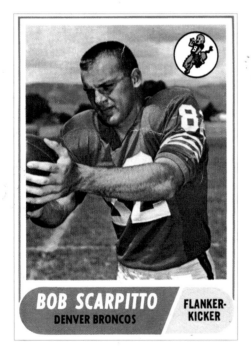

BOB SCARPITTO
DENVER BRONCOS
FLANKER-KICKER

Later, the bronco was pictured kicking its way through a big "D" without a rider. In 1997, the Broncos began using navy blue as their main uniform color. That year, the team also changed the look of the bronco, making it more stylish.

Bob Scarpitto wears the team's bright orange uniform for this 1960s trading card.

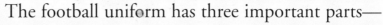

The football uniform has three important parts—

- Helmet
- Jersey
- Pants

Helmets used to be made out of leather, and they did not have facemasks—ouch! Today, helmets are made of super-strong plastic. The uniform top, or jersey, is made of thick fabric. It fits snugly around a player so that tacklers cannot grab it and pull him down. The pants come down just over the knees.

There is a lot more to a football uniform than what you see on the outside. Air can be pumped inside the helmet to give it a snug, padded fit. The jersey covers shoulder pads, and sometimes a rib-protector called a "flak jacket." The pants include pads that protect the hips, thighs, *tailbone*, and knees.

Football teams have two sets of uniforms— one dark and one light. This makes it easier to tell two teams apart on the field. Almost all teams wear their dark uniforms at home, and their light ones on the road.

Linebacker Al Wilson wears the Broncos' dark home uniform.

We Won!

The Broncos waited 14 seasons before they had their first winning record. Soon after that, however, they rose to the top of the **American Football Conference (AFC)**. In 1977, the Broncos won the AFC West and defeated the Pittsburgh Steelers and Oakland Raiders in the **playoffs** to become conference champions. Although they lost to the Cowboys 27–10 in Super Bowl XII, "Broncomania" was born.

Denver won the **AFC Championship** again in 1986, 1987, and 1989. John Elway led the team to amazing playoff victories to reach the Super Bowl, but each time the team fell one win short of the championship. As Elway neared the end of his career, Denver fans feared they had missed their chance.

In 1995, Mike Shanahan was named head coach. He brought a new style to the team and surrounded Elway with players who made him an even better quarterback. In 1997, the Broncos were the best team in the AFC again. Elway threw for 27 touchdowns and running back Terrell Davis gained 1,750 yards. Nine times that season, Denver scored more than 30 points in a game.

That January, the Broncos faced Brett Favre and the Green Bay Packers in Super Bowl XXXII. With the Packers worried about

Terrell Davis leaves a Green Bay tackler in the grass during Super Bowl XXXII.

Elway and his receivers, Davis was able to find plenty of running room in the Green Bay defense, and he gained 157 yards. The game was tied 24–24 late in the fourth quarter when Davis scored his third touchdown. Favre drove his team into Denver territory, but the Broncos **batted down** two desperate passes to win 31–24. More than 600,000 fans attended a parade for the champions in Denver two days later.

The victory over the Packers was just the beginning for the Broncos. They were even better the following season. They won their first 13 games in 1998 and set a new team record by winning 14 games in all. Elway and Davis had great years again. Receivers Shannon Sharpe, Rod Smith, and Ed McCaffrey caught more than 200 passes and scored 26 touchdowns.

The Broncos faced the Atlanta Falcons in Super Bowl XXXIII. This time, the defense kept a careful eye on Davis. This opened up

the field for Elway, who passed for 336 yards. He threw for one touchdown and ran for another. Meanwhile, the Denver defense did not allow a touchdown until the end of the game. By then it was too late for Atlanta. The Broncos won 34–19. It was the first time in almost 20 years that the same team had won the Super Bowl twice in a row.

LEFT: John Elway is carried off the field after beating the Green Bay Packers.
ABOVE: John Elway sneaks across the goal line during Super Bowl XXXIII.

Go-To Guys

To be a true star in the NFL, you need more than fast feet and a big body. You have to be a "go-to guy"—someone the coach wants on the field at the end of a big game. Broncos fans have had a lot to cheer about over the years, including these great stars…

THE PIONEERS

LIONEL TAYLOR   Wide Receiver

• BORN: 8/15/1935 • PLAYED FOR TEAM: 1960 TO 1966

Lionel Taylor was the team's first star. He led the AFL in **receiving** in five of the league's first six seasons.

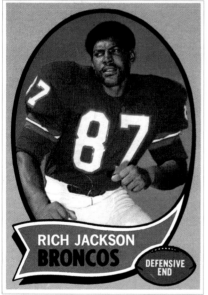

RICH JACKSON
BRONCOS
DEFENSIVE END

RICH JACKSON   Defensive End

• BORN: 7/22/1941
• PLAYED FOR TEAM: 1967 TO 1972

Rich Jackson was nicknamed "Tombstone" because he "buried" opposing quarterbacks. He was the first Bronco to be a first-team NFL All-Pro, which means he was the best player in football at his position.

FLOYD LITTLE

Running Back

- BORN: 7/4/1942
- PLAYED FOR TEAM: 1967 TO 1975

Floyd Little was called "The *Franchise*" by Broncos fans because, for many years, he was the whole team. He was Denver's best all-time player until John Elway starred for the team in the 1980s.

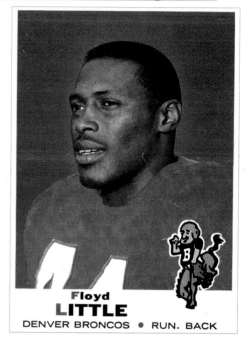

Floyd
LITTLE
DENVER BRONCOS • RUN. BACK

RANDY GRADISHAR   Linebacker

- BORN: 3/3/1952
- PLAYED FOR TEAM: 1974 TO 1983

Randy Gradishar was everything you could ask a linebacker to be. He was always in the right place at the right time, and never missed a game during his career.

TOM JACKSON

Linebacker

- BORN: 4/4/1951   • PLAYED FOR TEAM: 1973 TO 1986

Tom Jackson was the heart and soul of Denver's "Orange Crush" defense. He was smaller and slower than other linebackers, but he always found a way to get the job done.

LEFT: Rich Jackson   **ABOVE**: Floyd Little

MODERN STARS

JOHN ELWAY   Quarterback

• BORN: 6/28/1960   • PLAYED FOR TEAM: 1983 TO 1998

John Elway was one of the most talented quarterbacks in history. He could throw touchdown passes from anywhere on the field, and no one was cooler under pressure.

KARL MECKLENBURG   Linebacker

• BORN: 9/1/1960   • PLAYED FOR TEAM: 1983 TO 1994

More than 350 players were chosen in 1983 before the Broncos called Karl Mecklenburg's name in the **college draft**. Once he got a chance to prove himself, he became one of the best defensive players in the NFL.

STEVE ATWATER   Safety

• BORN: 10/28/1966

• PLAYED FOR TEAM: 1989 TO 1998

No one tackled harder than Steve Atwater, who roamed the field like an extra linebacker for the Broncos. He was selected to play in the **Pro Bowl** seven seasons in a row.

SHANNON SHARPE　　　　　　　　　　　Tight End

- BORN: 6/26/1968
- PLAYED FOR TEAM:
  1990 TO 1999 &
  2002 TO 2003

Shannon Sharpe was one of the most talkative players in the NFL. He backed up his words by becoming one of the most dangerous pass-catchers ever to play tight end.

TERRELL DAVIS　　　　　　　　　　　Running Back

- BORN: 10/28/1972　• PLAYED FOR TEAM: 1995 TO 2001

Terrell Davis won a lifelong battle with **_migraine headaches_** to become the best runner in team history. He was fast and powerful, and it often took two or three players to tackle him. Davis ran for 2,008 yards and 21 touchdowns in 1998, and was named NFL Offensive Player of the Year.

ROD SMITH　　　　　　　　　　　Wide Receiver

- BORN: 5/15/1970　• FIRST SEASON WITH TEAM: 1995

Rod Smith became a great receiver because he ran his **patterns** precisely and almost never dropped a pass. His hard work and dedication resulted in 113 catches during the 2001 season.

LEFT: Steve Atwater　　**ABOVE**: Shannon Sharpe

On the Sidelines

A smart coach can make a good football team great, and a great team unbeatable. This has certainly been true in the case of the Broncos. During the 1970s, John Ralston built a powerful defensive team. Red Miller, his **offensive coordinator**, took over the Broncos in 1977 and the team made it to the Super Bowl.

Denver's next coach was Dan Reeves. He learned the game from Tom Landry of the Dallas Cowboys, who demanded discipline and focus. Reeves asked nothing less of the Broncos, and they went to the Super Bowl three times while he was on the sidelines.

The Broncos did not win a Super Bowl until Mike Shanahan took over in the 1990s. He knew how to get the most out of his players, and created **game plans** around their skills. Shanahan was especially good at *analyzing* an opponent's defense. Many experts have called him a football genius.

There is no question that Mike Shanahan is the boss on the Denver sidelines.

One Great Day

Everyone in Denver knew they were getting a good young quarterback when the Broncos traded for John Elway after the 1983 draft. In the seasons that followed, they waited patiently for him to become a *winning* quarterback. During Elway's first three years with the Broncos, he threw more **interceptions** than touchdowns, and failed to win a playoff game. The fans were starting to lose their patience.

In 1986, Elway finally had the season everyone had been expecting. He threw for 3,485 yards and 19 touchdowns. The Broncos finished first in the AFC West, and Elway beat the New England Patriots in the playoffs to set up a *showdown* with the Cleveland Browns in the AFC Championship.

Playing in Cleveland on a cold January day, the Broncos led the game 13–10 in the fourth quarter. With the home crowd behind them, the Browns stormed back to score 10 points and take a 20–13 lead. Elway had time enough for one last **drive**. Starting on his own 2 yard line, he led the Broncos on an amazing 98-yard touchdown march that sent the game into **overtime**.

26

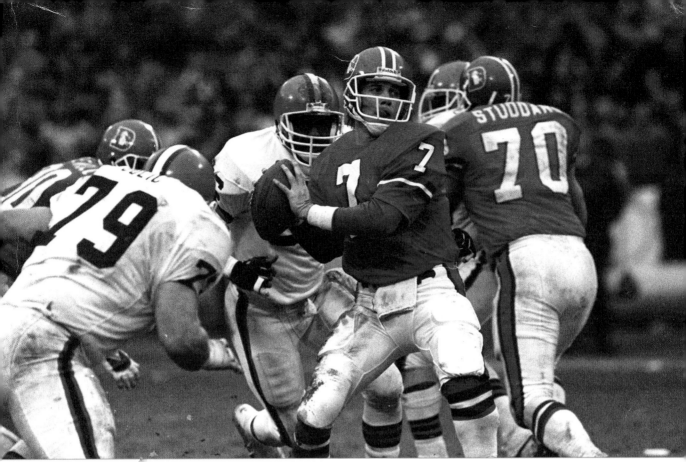

John Elway fires a pass against the Browns during "The Drive."

In overtime, the Denver defense stopped the Browns' first drive and forced them to punt. Elway, now full of confidence, completed two long passes. With the ball on Cleveland's 16 yard line, kicker Rich Karlis came into the game and booted the winning **field goal**.

The Broncos would win five AFC Championships with Elway at quarterback. He would perform many more remarkable feats, but his 98-yard *masterpiece* would forever be known by Broncos fans as "The Drive."

Legend Has It

Who wore the ugliest socks in football?

LEGEND HAS IT that the Broncos did. Football socks are either one solid color, or a mix of *horizontal* stripes. In the early 1960s, the Broncos wore socks with brown vertical stripes. The players and fans complained, but the team did not get different socks until 1962. When the new socks arrived, the players made a pile of the old ones and set it on fire.

Do the Broncos have football's greatest home-field advantage?

LEGEND HAS IT that they do. Because their field is one mile above sea level, the air is "thinner." During games, footballs travel slightly farther on passes and kicks. Sometimes this catches visiting players by surprise. The greatest advantage comes at the end of games, when opponents often have trouble catching their breath. Because the Broncos practice at this *altitude*, their bodies are used to the difference.

Tom Jackson, the leader of the Orange Crush defense,
stretches before a game.

Where did Denver's "Orange Crush" defense get its nickname?

LEGEND HAS IT that it came from a brand of soda. During the 1970s, the Broncos were one of the hardest-tackling teams in the NFL. Time and again, ball carriers were crushed by Denver players wearing bright orange jerseys. There was a soft drink called Orange Crush that was very popular at the time, so the fans simply "borrowed" it as a team nickname. The soda company was happy for the free advertising.

It Really Happened

Snowstorms are a part of life when you live in Denver. Indeed, the Broncos have sloshed their way through cold, wintry weather many times. Still, no one was prepared for what happened in late October of 1997, when a blizzard dumped 22 inches of snow on the city. It was the worst storm in Denver in nearly 30 years.

The blizzard hit on a Friday, the same day the Broncos were supposed to fly to Buffalo for a game against the Bills. Denver International Airport came to a halt. Planes could not take off, and thousands of people had to sleep in chairs and on the floor. No one could drive out of Denver, because the roads were a mess.

Many Broncos got in their cars and tried to drive to the airport or to the team's headquarters. They found themselves stranded in **snow banks** all over the city. When fans heard about this, they formed snowmobile patrols and picked up the players. On Saturday, the team's jet was able to take off, with the entire team on board.

The Broncos were exhausted when they took the field against the Bills the next day. Some players joked that they did not care what happened, as long as the game did not go into overtime. Of course, that is *just* what happened—after 60 minutes, the game was tied 20–20!

Denver fans are used to the snow. They came to the rescue
when the team needed them most.

The Broncos *summoned* what little strength they had left, and
ended up winning 23–20. When the players got back to Denver, they
were happy to see blue skies and plowed roads. It was nice to know
that they wouldn't have to take snowmobiles home.

Team Spirit

Few teams in professional football have fans as *passionate* and supportive as the Broncos. People in Colorado are crazy about their team. More than one million fans lined the streets of Denver for the parades celebrating the team's Super Bowl victories during the 1990s.

For home games in Denver, it is almost impossible to get a ticket. They sell out long before the season even starts. Inside the stadium, the fans are so loud that opposing players have to scream to talk to each other. The crowd noise is known as "Rocky Mountain Thunder."

Thunder also happens to be the name of the Denver mascot. Thunder is an Arabian *stallion*. Every time the Broncos score a touchdown, he charges on to the field. Going to a game in Denver is an experience fans never forget.

Rain or shine, the fans of the Denver Broncos are ready to root for their team.

Timeline

In this timeline, each Super Bowl is listed under the year it was played. Remember that the Super Bowl is held early in the year, and is actually part of the previous season. For example, Super Bowl XL was played on February 4 of 2006, but it was the championship of the 2005 NFL season.

1960
The Broncos play their first season.

1978
The Broncos reach the Super Bowl for the first time.

1962
Gene Mingo leads the AFL in field goals for the second time.

1965
Lionel Taylor becomes first AFL receiver with 500 catches.

1973
Coach John Ralston leads the Broncos to their first winning season.

Gene Mingo

Lionel Taylor

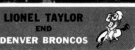

LIONEL TAYLOR
END
DENVER BRONCOS

A championship pennant
sold at Super Bowl XXI.

Terrell Davis
challenges the
Green Bay
defense in Super
Bowl XXXII.

1987
The Broncos win their second
AFC Championship.

1998
The Broncos beat the
Green Bay Packers to win
Super Bowl XXXII.

1983
The Broncos trade
for John Elway.

1990
The Broncos reach the
Super Bowl for the third
time in four seasons.

1999
John Elway retires
after beating the
Atlanta Falcons in
Super Bowl
XXXIII.

John Elway waves
goodbye to the fans.

35

Fun Facts

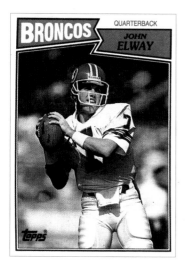

NAME OF THE GAME

John Elway led the Broncos to so many comeback victories that opponents actually had a name for getting beaten by him: "Getting Elwayed."

WORKING OVERTIME

In 1974, the Broncos played in the first regular-season overtime game in NFL history. At the end of **regulation time**, Denver and the Pittsburgh Steelers were tied at 35-35. Neither team scored in the sudden death period, so the game was declared a tie.

LIKE FATHER, LIKE SON

Frank Tripucka played quarterback for the Broncos from 1960 to 1964. His son, Kelly, also chose a career in professional sports—as a basketball player. He was a star for 10 seasons in the National Basketball Association.

MINGO MANIA

Gene Mingo was one of Denver's most popular players in the early 1960s. He did a little bit of everything—running the football, catching passes, and returning kicks. Mingo's greatest skill was kicking the football. He led the AFL in field goals and points in 1960 and 1962. Mingo was also the first African-American to be a full-time **place kicker** in the pros.

FLYING HIGH

Austin William "Goose" Gonsoulin set a team record with 11 interceptions in Denver's first season in 1960.

GOOSE GONSOULIN DEFENSIVE BACK DENVER BRONCOS

GOOD FRIENDS, GREAT HANDS

Mark Jackson, Vance Johnson, and Ricky Nattiel were best buddies and star receivers for the Broncos in the 1980s. They were nicknamed "The Three Amigos" after the 1986 movie starring Steve Martin.

LEFT TOP: John Elway
LEFT BOTTOM: Frank Tripucka   **ABOVE**: "Goose" Gonsoulin

Talking Football

Mike Shanahan

"If you're not improving… chances are you're not going to win."
— *Mike Shanahan, on the secret to success in football*

"You can be the best person in the league but if you don't win championships, something's missing."
— *Terrell Davis, on the thrill of winning the Super Bowl*

"Practice, dedication, and sacrifice. These are the keys to success… It will take time, but it's worth it."
— *John Elway, on what it takes to win a Super Bowl*

Dan Reeves leans on one of the giant "medicine balls"
football teams use to build strength.

"Difficulties in life are intended to make us better, not bitter."

—*Dan Reeves, on overcoming adversity*

For the Record

The great Broncos teams and players have left their marks on the record books. These are the "best of the best"…

Craig Morton

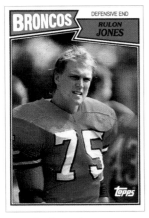

Rulon Jones

BRONCOS AWARD WINNERS

WINNER	AWARD	YEAR
Billy Joe	AFL Rookie of the Year	1963
Willie Brown	AFL All-Star Game MVP	1964
John Ralston	AFC Coach of the Year	1973
Craig Morton	Comeback Player of the Year	1977
Craig Morton	AFC Most Valuable Player	1977
Red Miller	NFL Coach of the Year	1977
Randy Gradishar	NFL Defensive Player of the Year	1978
Rulon Jones	AFC Defensive Most Valuable Player	1986
John Elway	AFC Offensive Most Valuable Player	1987
Dan Reeves	AFC Coach of the Year	1989
Mike Croel	AFC Rookie of the Year	1991
Dan Reeves	AFC Coach of the Year	1991
John Elway	AFC Offensive Most Valuable Player	1993
Terrell Davis	AFC Offensive Most Valuable Player	1996
Terrell Davis	NFL Offensive Player of the Year	1996
Terrell Davis	Super Bowl XXXII MVP	1997
Terrell Davis	NFL Offensive Player of the Year	1998
John Elway	Super Bowl XXXIII MVP	1998
Mike Anderson	NFL Offensive Rookie of the Year	2000
Clinton Portis	NFL Offensive Rookie of the Year	2002

BRONCOS ACHIEVEMENTS

ACHIEVEMENT	YEAR
AFC West Champions	1977
AFC Champions	1977
AFC West Champions	1978
AFC West Champions	1984
AFC West Champions	1986
AFC Champions	1986
AFC West Champions	1987
AFC Champions	1987
AFC West Champions	1989
AFC Champions	1989
AFC West Champions	1991
AFC West Champions	1996
AFC Champions	1997
Super Bowl XXXII Champions	1997*
AFC Champions	1998
Super Bowl XXXIII Champions	1998*
AFC West Champions	2005

Super Bowls are played early the following year, but the game is counted as the championship of this season.

ABOVE: Quarterback John Elway celebrates another touchdown.

BELOW: This pennant celebrates Denver's 1987 AFC Championship. It was sold at Super Bowl XXII in San Diego, California.

Pinpoints

The history of a football team is made up of many smaller stories. These stories take place all over the map—not just in the city a team calls "home." Match the push-pins on these maps to the Team Facts and you will begin to see the story of the Broncos unfold!

TEAM FACTS

1   Denver, Colorado—*The Broncos play their home games here.*

2   San Diego, California—*Terrell Davis was born here.*

3   Port Angeles, Washington—*John Elway was born here.*

4   Luling, Texas—*Riley Odoms was born here.*

5   New Orleans, Louisiana—*The Broncos played in their first Super Bowl here.*

6   Texarkana, Arkansas—*Rod Smith was born here.*

7   Miami, Florida—*The Broncos won Super Bowl XXXIII here.*

8   Warren, Ohio—*Randy Gradishar was born here.*

9   Chicago, Illinois—*Otis Armstrong was born here.*

10   New Haven, Connecticut—*Floyd Little was born here.*

11   London, England—*The Broncos played in the 1987* **American Bowl** *here.*

12   Tokyo, Japan—*The Broncos played in the 1990 American Bowl here.*

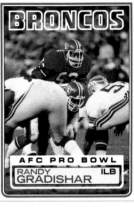

Randy Gradishar

Play Ball

Football is a sport played by two teams on a field that is 100 yards long. The game is divided into four 15-minute quarters. Each team must have 11 players on the field at all times. The group that has the ball is called the offense. The group trying to keep the offense from moving the ball forward is called the defense.

A football game is made up of a series of "plays." Each play starts and ends with a referee's signal. A play begins when the center snaps the ball between his legs to the quarterback. The quarterback then gives the ball to a teammate, throws (or "passes") the ball to a teammate, or runs with the ball himself. The job of the defense is to tackle the player with the ball or stop the quarterback's pass. A play ends when the ball (or player holding the ball) is "down." The offense must move the ball forward at least 10 yards every four downs. If it fails to do so, the other team is given the ball. If the offense has not made 10 yards after three downs—and does not want to risk losing the ball—it can kick (or "punt") the ball to make the other team start from its own end of the field.

At each end of a football field is a goal line, which divides the field from the end zone. A team must run or pass the ball over the goal line to score a touchdown, which counts for six points. After scoring a touchdown, a team can try a short kick for one "extra point," or try again to run or pass across the goal line for two points. Teams can score three points from anywhere on the field by kicking the ball between the goal posts. This is called a field goal.

The defense can score two points if it tackles a player while he is in his own end zone. This is called a safety. The defense can also score points by taking the ball away from the offense and crossing the opposite goal line for a touchdown. The team with the most points after 60 minutes is the winner.

Football may seem like a very hard game to understand, but the more you play and watch football, the more "little things" you are likely to notice. The next time you are at a game, look for these plays:

PLAY LIST

BLITZ—A play where the defense sends extra tacklers after the quarterback. If the quarterback sees a blitz coming, he passes the ball quickly. If he does not, he can end up on the bottom of a very big pile!

DRAW—A play where the offense pretends it will pass the ball, and then gives it to a running back. If the offense can "draw" the defense to the quarterback and his receivers, the running back should have lots of room to run.

FLY PATTERN—A play where a team's fastest receiver is told to "fly" past the defensive backs for a long pass. Many long touchdowns are scored on this play.

SQUIB KICK—A play where the ball is kicked a short distance on purpose. A squib kick is used when the team kicking off does not want the other team's fastest player to catch the ball and run with it.

SWEEP—A play where the ball-carrier follows a group of teammates moving sideways to "sweep" the defense out of the way. A good sweep gives the runner a chance to gain a lot of yards before he is tackled or forced out of bounds.

Glossary

AFC CHAMPIONSHIP—The game that decides which American Football Conference team will play in the Super Bowl.

AMERICAN BOWL—A preseason game played by two NFL teams in a foreign city.

AMERICAN FOOTBALL CONFERENCE (AFC)—One of two groups of teams that make up the National Football League (NFL). The winner of the AFC plays the winner of the National Football Conference (NFC) in the Super Bowl.

AMERICAN FOOTBALL LEAGUE (AFL)—The football league that began play in 1960, and later merged with the National Football League (NFL).

BLOCKERS—Players who use their bodies to protect the ball carrier.

COLLEGE DRAFT—The meeting at which NFL teams take turns choosing the best college players each year.

DRIVE—A series of plays that drives the defense back toward its own goal.

FIELD GOAL—A goal from the field, kicked over the crossbar and between the goal posts. A field goal is worth three points.

FRANCHISE—One of many teams that are "partners" in the same league.

GAME PLANS—A set of instructions for players to follow in each game.

INTERCEPTIONS—Passes caught by the defensive team.

OFFENSIVE COORDINATOR—The coach who is in charge of planning a team's offensive plays.

OVERTIME—The period played to decide the winner of a game that is tied after 60 minutes. This period is sometimes called "sudden death" because the game ends as soon as one team scores.

PATTERNS—The path a receiver follows while trying to get open on a pass play.

PLACE KICKER—A player whose job is to kick field goals and extra points.

PLAYOFFS—The games played after the season that determine which teams meet in the Super Bowl.

PROFESSIONAL—A person or team that plays a sport for money. College players are not paid, so they are considered "amateurs."

PRO BOWL—The NFL's All-Star Game, played after the Super Bowl.

RECEIVING—Catching passes from the quarterback. Each pass caught counts as one reception.

REGULATION TIME—The amount of time (60 minutes) that the rules allow for an official game.

SPECIAL TEAMS—Groups of players who take the field for special plays, including kickoffs, punts, and field goals.

SUPER BOWL—The championship game of football, played between the winner of the American Football Conference (AFC) and the National Football Conference (NFC).

OTHER WORDS TO KNOW

ALTITUDE—The height of something above sea level.

ANALYZING—Separating into small parts and studying closely.

BATTED DOWN—Knocked out of the air with the arms or hands.

EXECUTIVE—A person who makes important decisions in a business.

FIBERGLASS—A building material made with fine threads of glass.

HORIZONTAL—Going from side to side.

INCORPORATES—Includes in part of a larger thing.

MASTERPIECE—An artist's best or most famous work.

MIGRAINE HEADACHES—Severe headaches that cause great pain and affect vision.

PASSIONATE—Having strong emotions.

SHOWDOWN—A meeting to decide something once and for all.

SNOW BANKS—Large piles of snow created by the wind, or by snowplows.

STALLION—A male horse.

SUMMONED—Called up or stirred up.

TAILBONE—The bone that protects the base of the spine.

TRADITION— A belief or custom that is handed down from generation to generation.

Places to Go

ON THE ROAD

INVESCO FIELD AT MILE HIGH
1701 Bryant St
Denver, Colorado 80204
(720) 258-3000

THE PRO FOOTBALL HALL OF FAME
2121 George Halas Drive NW
Canton, Ohio 44708
(330) 456-8207

ON THE WEB

THE NATIONAL FOOTBALL LEAGUE   www.nfl.com
   • *Learn more about the National Football League*

THE DENVER BRONCOS   www.DenverBroncos.com
   • *Learn more about the Denver Broncos*

THE PRO FOOTBALL HALL OF FAME   www.profootballhof.com
   • *Learn more about football's greatest players*

ON THE BOOKSHELF

To learn more about the sport of football, look for these books at your library or bookstore:

   • Fleder, Rob–Editor. *The Football Book*. New York, NY: Sports Illustrated Books, 2005.

   • Kennedy, Mike. *Football*. Danbury, CT: Franklin Watts, 2003.

   • Savage, Jeff. *Play by Play Football*. Minneapolis, MN: Lerner Sports, 2004.

Index

The Team

PAGE NUMBERS IN **BOLD** REFER TO ILLUSTRATIONS.

MARK STEWART has written more than 20 books on football, and over 100 sports books for kids. He grew up in New York City during the 1960s rooting for the Giants and Jets, and now takes his two daughters, Mariah and Rachel, to watch them play in their home state of New Jersey. Mark comes from a family of  writers. His grandfather was Sunday Editor of *The New York Times* and his mother was Articles Editor of *The Ladies Home Journal* and *McCall's*. Mark has profiled hundreds of athletes over the last 20 years. He has also written several books about New York and New Jersey. Mark is a graduate of Duke University, with a degree in history. He lives with his daughters and wife, Sarah, overlooking Sandy Hook, NJ.

JASON AIKENS is the Collections Curator at the Pro Football Hall of Fame. He is responsible for the preservation of the Pro Football Hall of Fame's collection of artifacts and memorabilia and obtaining new donations of memorabilia from current players and NFL teams. Jason has a Bachelor of Arts in History from Michigan State University and a Masters in History from Western Michigan University where he concentrated on sports history. Jason has been working for the Pro Football Hall of Fame since 1997; before that he was an intern at the College Football Hall of Fame. Jason's family has roots in California  and has been following the St. Louis Rams since their days in Los Angeles, California. He lives with his wife Cynthia and recent addition to the team Angelina in Canton, OH.